SUPERSTITIOUS? HERE'S WHY!

JULIE FORSYTH BATCHELOR
CLAUDIA DE LYS

Superstitious?
Here's Why!

Illustrated by Erik Blegvad

NEW YORK

HARCOURT, BRACE & WORLD, INC.

LIBRARY OF CONGRESS CATALOG CARD NUMBER: 54-8566

PRINTED IN THE UNITED STATES OF AMERICA

Contents

"Come on, superstition, and get my goat.
  I got mascots.
  The stars of my birthday favor me.
  The numbers from one to ten are with me.
I was born under a lucky star and nothing can stop me.
The moon was a waxing moon and not a waning moon
  when I was born.
Every card in the deck and both of the seven-eleven
  bones are with me.
So you hear them tell it and they mean if it works it's
  good and if it don't it costs nothing."

FROM *The People, Yes* BY CARL SANDBURG

Introduction

Superstitions were part of the language and background of most of us as children. We learned them from our parents and playmates. Through the years, many of these beliefs became habits of thought and action. To "knock on wood" after making a prediction, or to toss spilt salt over the left shoulder seem the natural things to do.

But how did these superstitions begin? And what was the reason for them? To find the origin of most of those familiar beliefs, sayings, and customs of today we must travel back into the folklore of the past.

There is every reason to believe that the earliest superstitions grew out of pagan religions. Sun-worship and moon-worship were very important to primitive man. These heavenly bodies were viewed with great fear and respect, and it was believed both had the power to change human affairs. So thousands of beliefs sprang up about them.

These savage ancestors of ours were not stupid. In fact, most were more observant than people are today. With absolutely no knowledge about the laws of nature and man, they were constantly trying to figure out what made things happen. Everything was a mystery—lightning, shooting stars, eclipses, birth, and death, to mention a few of them. So there was always the question "Why?"; and, always, the fear of the unknown.

Early man's close observation led to a strong belief in unseen spirits. He saw that animals seemed to hear and sense things men couldn't. These must be ghosts or supernatural beings, he reasoned. Such things as the miracles of trees growing from tiny seeds and tadpoles becoming frogs also seemed to indicate help from invisible spirits.

Since life in those times was so difficult, primitive man assumed that there were many more bad spirits than good ones. The question was how to protect oneself, and how to appease these evil powers. So they invented all sorts of charms, amulets and talismans, as well as every kind of counter-magic. When one failed they tried another. That's why today we have dozens of counter-charms to break each spell or jinx early man imagined.

There's scarcely a thing in man's environment about which a superstition hasn't been woven. Sometimes there was a sensible reason behind it. At other times man's intense curiosity about the world led him to beliefs that were half-truths.

Our ancestors were sure that inanimate objects as well as humans had both good and evil powers. If a rock fell they thought it had a reason for falling. When two people said the same word at the same time, it was never a coincidence but a sign to make a wish.

Many superstitions were based on "wishful thinking." The ancients expected a wish to come true if made while looking at or touching something connected with good fortune. This was sympathetic magic, or "like brings like."

A favorite counter-charm was to do something in reverse, or to say something that was just the opposite of what you wanted. This was supposed to change bad luck to good luck. The instinct of trying to equalize the positive and the negative has been found among all the peoples of the world.

Saliva was popular as counter-magic. Probably when early man discovered it was able to change the nature of food in the mouth he believed it must have other "magical" powers. After deciding that saliva might be a protection against evil, it was but a step further to think it could dissolve bad luck.

Thus superstitions grew, almost all of them based on ignorance and fear. Each country added its beliefs and old wives' tales.

It must be granted that there often seems to be an element of luck at work, either good or bad. And we know that many people who have a strong faith can often make what they believe in come to pass. Therefore, despite facts and logic, the belief in good or bad luck influences the thoughts and actions of many people today.

POWER OF SUGGEST.

If carrying a rabbit's foot gives you confidence and faith in yourself, keep one in your pocket. But recognize it for what it is—a prop, that only has the power your thinking gives it. Remember, too, that superstitions offer an immature individual an excuse for blaming some power beyond himself for his bad fortune. But instead of fighting these beliefs with scientific law let's view them with tolerance and amusement. For they are wonderful whimsy, and the stuff of which dreams are made.

SUPERSTITIOUS? HERE'S WHY!

Charms

Four-leaf Clover

There's a traditional saying that goes like this:

> One leaf for fame,
> One leaf for wealth,
> And one leaf for a faithful lover,
> And one leaf to bring glorious health,
> Are all in a four-leaf clover!

Many are the legends about the power of this small plant. One is that Eve took a four-leaf clover with her when she was cast out of the Garden of Eden. So it was considered a rare plant indeed, and a very lucky sign if any were found growing in one's garden.

However, long before the tale of Adam and Eve, the Druids of England, who were sun-worshipers, believed the four-leaf clover to have magical powers; that whoever found one was able to see evil beings such as witches and devils, and therefore could avoid them.

According to other folklore, the origin of the four-leaf clover as a lucky symbol may have been that it looked like a cross. This is not the religious cross but one called the Solar or Sun Cross which primitive man used as a crude system of direction. One straight line stood for sunrise to sunset, or East to West. Another line represented North to South. The crossing of these formed the prehistoric Solar Cross. Later, the four lobes of the clover became known as North, South, East and West.

In Ireland, the four-leaf clover has been held in the same high regard as the three-lobed shamrock. A popular saying today, "He's in clover," means a person is playing in good luck.

Although the four-leaf clover is really a freak plant from the original three-leaf herb, it has been so in demand among millions of superstitious people that a seed has been developed which sprouts only four-leaf clovers. Now you can have a potful of luck on your window sill, or even a whole garden of it!

Carry an Acorn

For general good luck, or to insure a long life, many people carry an acorn. It may be a real one, or it's often made of gold, silver or other materials. Women wear them about their neck or on bracelets.

In Asia Minor, long ago, the acorn was sacred to the goddess of Nature. But the Scandinavians were of the opinion that the oak tree belonged to Thor, their god of thunder and lightning. As lightning was thought always to enter a house through a window, an acorn was placed there so Thor would spare the house.

Later, dried acorns were used as the knobs on window shade cords and superstitious housewives knitted or crocheted small covers for them. Still later, real acorns were replaced by ones made of wood.

While people today realize that acorns can bring no better luck than any other seed, there's still a great demand for these charms.

Hang Up a Horseshoe

There are many superstitions about the horseshoe and the good luck it brings when hanging over the doorway. All these beliefs are related to the symbols of the half-circle and crescent. Early religions considered crescent or U-shaped objects powerful and protective signs. In ancient Yucatan and Peru, temples were built with arched doorways because of this notion. In Spain the Moors designed their mosques in arch formation. Ruins at Stonehenge, England, show that the religious grounds of the sun-worshiping Druids were in semi-circles or horseshoe design. Down through the Middle Ages churches and public buildings were built with arched windows and doorways as a means of protection against evil.

It is thought that the first horseshoes were made by the Greeks during the 4th Century. Horses were held sacred at that time, so their crescent-shaped shoes became symbols of good luck. Added power came from the fact that horseshoes were made of iron, the metal that people believed protected one from witches. There was still a third factor for luck: horseshoes, until recent years, were made to hold seven nails—a mystic and potent number. So it's no wonder that the

Greeks and Romans always kept a horseshoe nailed to the wall for protection against almost anything.

An old wives' tale has it that when a horseshoe is hung with prongs up, the Devil is sucked in and destroyed if he gets too near; when prongs are down, the magic in the horseshoe pours out and keeps him from crossing the threshold. So, as far as luck is concerned, it doesn't seem to matter which way the prongs are placed. But be sure your horseshoe is nailed tightly, for if it falls on someone's head—that's bad luck!

Carry a Horse Chestnut

Carrying a horse chestnut, sometimes called a "buckeye," is supposed to relieve pains and cure a headache. Also it is thought, especially by children, to be a good luck charm.

The folklore concerning this nut began in the Far East, for the chestnut tree is a native of Tibet. There were many things that seemed to link this tree with the horse. When the leaves fall, a horseshoe-shaped scar is left on the twig. The buds of the tree resemble a horse's foot. A horse chestnut, when cut on the slant, shows a miniature picture of a horse's hock and foot, shoe and nails.

Along with all this, those keen-eyed ancestors of ours saw that this tree lived longer than most. Acting on the notion that "like produces like" chestnuts were fed to horses so that they also might have long, healthy lives. In time, these nuts came to be considered medicine for humans as well.

In this country the tree was given the name of "buckeye" since the partly opened pods of a horse chestnut look like the eyes of a deer. Ohio, where many of these trees grow, is known as the "Buckeye State."

Food

Salt

When you spill salt, do you quickly throw a pinch of it over your left shoulder? Have you tried to catch a bird by shaking salt on its tail? Do you take a box of salt as a present to a friend in his new home?

Of all subjects that superstitions have been built around the most outstanding is salt. Its unusual properties have puzzled and fascinated people in every part of the world. Today we understand the chemical reasons which enable salt to thaw snow but help to freeze icecream. The ancients, however, were positive salt was magic and had a dual nature to do good or evil!

Man probably first noticed salt when he saw animals near a salt-lick. When he tried some it tasted good. Then as he came to realize that salt could preserve food he began to imagine that it also had the power to protect him.

When he spilled salt he was sure that his guardian spirit had caused the accident to warn him of evil nearby. The general belief was that good spirits lived on the right side of the body and bad spirits on the left. So early man quickly threw a pinch of the salt over his left shoulder to bribe those spirits who were planning to harm him.

Also, in those early days, salt was a precious and scarce item in some regions. So the taboo against spilling salt was one of economy as well.

Since tears are salty, spilling salt meant sadness to many people. You still hear the old saying, "Help me to salt, help me to sorrow." A popular Norwegian belief is that as many tears will be shed as are needed to dissolve the salt spilled. In New England, spilled salt is thrown on the stove so as to dry up any tears quickly.

Faith in the magic of salt made people believe it was easy to catch a bird if his tail feathers were salted. In recent years it has been reported that birds flying close enough to the Great Salt Lake in Utah to be covered by the salty water are easily captured. We now know that it is the weight of the salt on their wings that keeps the bird from flying away, not the magic in it!

Salt as a present for a friend in his new home is a custom in many countries. Because of its lasting quality and the fact that it preserves food, salt is believed close to friendship. In ancient Greece a stranger was welcomed by having a pinch of salt placed in his right hand. In Eastern countries salt was put before strangers as a pledge of good will. Hungary has long had the custom of sprinkling the threshold of a new house with salt, so no witch or evil thing will enter.

It was believed by the Greeks and Romans that it was the salt in sea water that purified it. So they worshiped a goddess of salt who represented health. At birth, salt was placed on a child's tongue in the goddess's name, so as to insure long life, good health and protection. Some peoples still perform this ceremony.

Because of the scarcity of this mineral in ancient times, the Roman soldiers, officials and working people were often paid with salt. That pay was called "salarium" which came from the word for salt, "sal," and meant salt money. From this we get our word salary.

Today we still use some expressions of early origin based on the importance of salt. Among these are: "He's not worth his salt," "I'll take that with a grain of salt," and "He's the salt of the earth."

An Apple a Day

"An apple a day keeps the doctor away" is an old saying. But of course we know that apples have no magic power to prevent disease. However, scientific tests show that this fruit gives us a much needed mineral, potassium. So the saying has a grain of truth in it.

Apples play a happy role in some of our holidays. These customs go back to pagan ceremonies in honor of Pomona, Roman goddess of fruit trees. Ducking for apples is still fun on Hallowe'en and Thanksgiving. Apple seeds are used in telling fortunes concerning love and marriage. One way is to count them, saying, "He loves me, he loves me not."

The belief that a green apple causes stomach ache has been upset in recent years. It's claimed that if eaten slowly, and chewed enough to mix the fruit thoroughly with saliva, it will cause no discomfort.

Onions and Garlic

This doggerel is a favorite with many farmers:

> Onion's skin very thin,
> Mild winter coming in.
> Onion's skin thick and tough,
> Coming winter cold and rough.

Sometimes this belief works and sometimes not. For the onion cannot be relied upon to predict an entire season's weather.

The ancient Egyptians often took their sacred oaths with the right hand on an onion. They thought of this vegetable as a symbol of eternity because of its unusual formation—one sphere within another. Not only was the onion believed to keep all evil spirits away, but to ward off disease.

From these early beliefs have come some of today's superstitions: a piece of onion on a shelf will absorb all germs; cut onion will draw out the poison from a snakebite; slices of onion will stop an insect bite from paining; eating onions will help cure a cold.

Strangely enough, modern science regards the onion as not only a very healthful vegetable but one containing important chemical compounds. When isolated, these compounds are said to be able to fight germs in human beings. So it would seem that those early peoples sensed this when they suggested onions for warding off disease.

Garlic, because of its odor and the fact that it is a relative of the onion, was also used in folk medicine. This, too, has been closely studied by scientists who find that the vapor (not the odor) from crushed garlic will kill some bacteria. In remote days it was customary to string garlic buds together as a necklace to wear when sleeping. This was a charm against the Evil Eye. Today wherever garlic is raised it's still the custom to hang a wreath of it over the door for protection.

Eat Bread Crusts for Curly Hair

The original saying was, "If you eat bread crumbs your hair will curl."

Bread has been known as the "staff of life" from the beginning of time. To the early dwellers it was a symbol of the essentials of life: a mixture of water and grain that was attracted out of the soil of Mother Earth by the powerful sun. So bread was considered a sacred gift, and even crumbs were never thrown away lest the gods be angry!

Hair, too, was looked on with awe. In the days of sun-worship the rays of the sun were thought to be the sun-god's hair. Kings wore crowns as symbols of these rays. Human hair became associated with the "sun's hair" as people observed that it often crackled and gave off sparks when combed.

Curly hair was considered very lucky, as it was identified with the curve the sun makes in its travels. Primitive man felt that anyone with ringlets was well-protected by the sun-god. Even when straight, the first hair cut from a baby's head was rolled into a ringlet and placed in a safe place to help the child have a long life.

Some ancestor, believing in the importance of curly hair and of eating every crumb of bread must have started this well-known superstition. Today, however, the saying has been changed to, "Eat bread crusts for curly hair," probably so that crusts won't be wasted.

Passing bread is merely a polite gesture now but in early times it expressed a wish for good health and a long life. Bread wasn't cut then; each person broke off his own piece from the loaf instead. In the East, once a man had "broken bread" with another they were friends. Because bread was eaten at the Last Supper it came to have a religious significance, and later was offered in the form of wafers at the Communion ceremony.

Is Fish a Brain Food?

The belief in fish as a brain food began when a noted French chemist, Jean Dumas, around the middle of the last century, established the fact that fish is rich in phosphorus. About the same time it was proved that the brain, too, contains a large amount of phosphorus. Whereupon, the German philosopher of that day, Friedrich Büchner, declared, "Without phosphorus there is no thought."

Meanwhile, a Swiss zoologist teaching at Harvard, Louis Agassiz, endorsed the belief that since both contained phosphorus, fish should be good for the brain. Of course the fish industry liked this idea and promoted it. So today we have many people who firmly believe that fish is brain food.

However, there is no evidence that fish produces gray matter. It, like other wholesome food, provides vital elements for the body. But so far as the brain is concerned, one food is as good as another. And remember, during the time the brain has its most extraordinary development—from birth to the sixth year—a child is eating very little fish!

Farming by the Moon

The early days of farming were in the time of moon-worship. Probably it was observing the relation of the moon to tides that made the primitives believe the moon was the source of all moisture. Every liquid, from the sap of plants to the blood of living creatures, was believed controlled by the moon.

Also, this planet was man's first calendar, as periods of time were reckoned by the moon in those days. So it was natural that the changes, or phases, of the moon each month were used as signals for doing things. Many farmers today follow those early superstitions.

Planting in the "light of the moon" means in the time between the new and full moon. Planting in the "dark of the moon" refers to the period between the full and the new moon. Scientists, however, have different meanings for these terms. They think of the light phase of the moon as the time it's above the horizon—from dusk to midnight; and the dark phase as between midnight and dawn. Tests so far fail to show that planting by the moon makes any great difference in the size of crops.

The full moons of September and October are

called the "harvest moons." Because of their brilliance
early folk were sure they were a special gift to the
farmer from good spirits. The truth is that during
these two months the moon makes a smaller angle with
the horizon, and so is more radiant. In the Southern
Hemisphere this bright moonlight takes place in late
March and April.

Sounds

Sing Before Breakfast

Superstitions about singing at the beginning of the day were just for children at first. But through the years they came to apply to adults as well. Two popular sayings were: "If you sing before seven, you'll cry before eleven"; and, "If you sing before you eat, you'll cry before you sleep."

In the early days, parents frowned on a child who showed such a happy disposition as to sing early in the morning. This may have had its origin in ancient

Greece where it was thought most unlucky to show gaiety as the day began, when nothing had been done to earn it. This superstition also followed the idea that things often work in reverse. A child who sang in the early morning was tempting fate and might have to be whipped before the day was over.

Among adult superstitions nowadays are these: it's unlucky to sing in bed as that is too early in the day; if you sing before breakfast or at the table you'll be disappointed in love or business; anyone who sings while playing cards will lose the game. But if you unconsciously begin to sing in the bathtub, it's supposed to be a sign of very good luck.

Better Not Whistle!

An old proverb goes like this:

> A whistling girl and a crowing hen,
> Always come to no good end.

The ancient taboo against whistling is seen today in the following superstitions: a whistle in the house invites the Devil in; if little girls whistle they'll grow a beard; a whistle by anyone in a theater's dressing rooms means the show will have bad luck; whistling aboard a ship will raise a storm; misfortune will follow if reporters whistle in editorial rooms or if miners do so when underground; you're rude if you whistle when guests are present.

In tracing the origins of these taboos it must be remembered that early man gave meaning, as best he could, to all things that happened around him. If certain sounds seemed bad to him, then all "like sounds" were condemned. The snake's hiss when angry, the swishing sound of arrows that brought death, and the whistling, moaning noises of the wind were a few of these. Therefore any hissing or whistling sound was regarded as a sign of danger.

When man first found he could whistle he probably thought it a new way of signaling. But, he reasoned, evil spirits as well as people might answer his whistle. So whistling was forbidden! Later, it was thought that men who whistled were casting a spell over others.

In time, as man became more intelligent, he whistled for his dog, but he always snapped his fingers at the same time as counter-magic. Dog owners do this now, not aware of what it means.

The phrase "You can whistle for it" still indicates that the chances are you won't get what you've asked for.

Today whistling, despite the many superstitions, is popular. It can show self-satisfaction in your work.

It gives you courage when you're alone or frightened. One variety of whistling shows surprise, while another indicates approval of a pretty girl.

Does a Dog's Howl Mean Death?

When a dog throws back its head and howls, especially at night, many feel sure that a death will occur. To certain primitives the howling dog was a symbol of the wind-god who was supposed to summon Death, and then carry away the spirits of the dead. To others, the dog was felt to have the power to see invisible demons since it had so many uncanny instincts for detecting enemies and locating prey. Just another example of man trying to explain something that puzzled and awed him!

Even today there are people who think that the dog actually sees the figure of Death and shows this by howling. The scientific reason for these howls is very simple. Wolves and wild dogs never bark or wag their tails, but howl they do. No doubt certain sounds, such as the moaning of the night or high-pitched musical notes, irritate a wolf's or a dog's very sensitive ears and it shows this by howling. A dog when it howls is acting according to instincts inherited from its wild ancestors, not giving a warning as some believe.

Reflexes

Yawning

We cover our mouths when yawning today because it's good manners to do so. But once upon a time, people put their hands over their mouths so they wouldn't lose their breath and die. They'd observed that one of the first things a newborn baby does is to yawn. So they knew this had something to do with breath and concluded it had to do with life itself.

During the Middle Ages it was a common belief that yawning was caused by the Devil so he could enter the body through the mouth. The counter-charm was to make the sign of the cross over the mouth. Many still do this, unaware of the reason the gesture is made.

Most Hindus think a yawn foretells danger. So they snap their fingers three times and call aloud on a divinity to protect them. Snapping the fingers three times is supposed to triple the chances of the divinity helping them.

Now we know that yawning may come from many causes. You often yawn if you are sleepy, bored, nervous, not breathing deeply enough, or if you see someone else yawn.

It's the custom today to apologize after yawning. This came from the ancients, but they did so because they felt a yawn meant danger and that anyone who "caught" it was in danger too. It's true that "a yawn is catching," but only because some unconscious signal seems to go from the sight center of the brain to the yawn center which promptly responds.

Sneezing

When you sneeze friends are apt to say, "God bless you," or the German expression, "Gesundheit," or perhaps the Italian word, "Felicità." Maybe they will merely follow the old practice, still popular in the

Near and Far East, of clasping their hands and bowing toward you.

The custom of asking God's blessing began when
early man believed that the essence of life—the spirit
or soul—was in the form of air or breath and resided
in one's head. A sneeze might accidentally expel the
spirit for a short time or even forever, unless God pre-
vented it. The act of bowing toward the sneezer was
also counter-magic. For it meant, "May your soul not
escape."

There were some ancients who believed that evil
spirits which had previously entered the body jumped
out when one sneezed. This meant danger to others
for such spirits might now enter their bodies. So the
expression or blessing was to protect others as well as
the one who sneezed. So serious was a sneeze considered in the Middle Ages that even today we speak
of certain situations as "not to be sneezed at."

Many superstitious people quote these lines:

> Sneeze on Monday, sneeze for danger;
> Sneeze on Tuesday, kiss a stranger;
> Sneeze on Wednesday, receive a letter;
> Sneeze on Thursday, something better;
> Sneeze on Friday, sneeze for sorrow;
> Sneeze on Saturday, see your lover tomorrow;
> Sneeze on Sunday, your safety seek
> Or the Devil will have you for the rest of the week.

Today we know that a sneeze is one of our unconscious reflexes. However, medical men consider it almost as harmful to others as some of the primitive people did. For, instead of "evil spirits," sneezing expels harmful bacteria and is one of the most effective ways of spreading disease. So your best countercharm, say the doctors, is to cover a sneeze with a handkerchief so your germs won't jump down someone else's throat.

Hiccoughing

The favorite explanation, in early days, of anything unpleasant was the Evil Eye. Having no idea what caused one to hiccough even civilized peoples blamed it on this.

"Cures" for hiccoughs ran into the hundreds and some are still practiced today. Oddly enough, two remedies used by the Orientals since remote times have a scientific basis. They are: drinking nine swallows of water without breathing; pressing a spot at the base of the neck. Each produces pressure on the phrenic nerve which in turn often relieves the hiccoughing impulse.

Another method of relief, that of breathing in and out while holding a paper bag over one's face with the opening covering the nose and mouth, also is scientific. As the bag fills with carbon dioxide it stimulates normal breathing reflexes in the lungs and frequently stops the hiccoughs.

Besides indigestion, hiccoughs can be caused by worry, fear or excitement. Almost anything that snaps the tension will relieve them. Hence the popular method of "scaring people out of hiccoughs" often works.

Babies may hiccough several months before they are born. It is now known that this is due to certain foods the mother eats to which the unborn child is allergic.

Birds

A Little Bird Told Me

In answer to "How did you find out?" the reply often is, "A little bird told me." This is only one of hundreds of superstitious ideas that relate birds to human beings. It stems from the very early belief that birds had a speech of their own, and could bring information to people. Both the Old Testament and the Koran (the bible of the Mohammedans) contain verses that indicate that birds were able to talk and give messages.

Birds are the world's best ventriloquists. Their notes may appear to come from far or near, when the birds are standing only ten feet from a listener. In ancient times, a few men mastered this difficult trick. They used it to mystify others, pretending to report divine messages. This led to the idea that wise men could speak and understand the languages of birds. So when they said, "A little bird told me," people were awed and readily believed them.

Birds were believed to be the messengers of departed souls or spirits. This was probably due to their flying up into the sky where spirits were thought to reside. When a bird tapped on the window or flew into a house, it was assumed that some spirit had come back to invite another to join him—in other words, a sign of death. This childish notion is still so strong that many persons refuse to have wallpaper in their homes which has a bird design on it.

Even down through the Middle Ages, the flight and behavior of birds was a great mystery. Not having today's means of studying migration, people were sure some birds hibernated in the ground during winter. While we've proved this to be false, we still don't know what gives these little creatures the signal to migrate.

Storks and Babies

The expression "the stork came" announces the birth of a baby in many countries. Early legends associated the stork with faithfulness in marriage, home-life, and birth. And rightly so! Probably no bird, unless it be the swan, is more devoted to its mate and takes better care of its family. Storks may live to be over seventy. Since they return each year to build a nest in the same chimney their habits have been studied for centuries, especially in Germany and Scandinavia where storks reside in great numbers.

High regard for this unusual bird went back at least to 330 B.C., when Aristotle wrote that it was a crime to kill a stork in northern Greece. It was believed this bird protected homes from lightning and other evil spirits.

The Romans thought so highly of the stork's behavior toward its family that they passed the famous "Stork's Law," called Lex Ciconaria. This compelled children to take care of their needy parents in old age.

Do Scarecrows Scare Crows?

A scarecrow is a picturesque sight in many cornfields and garden plots. Yet most farmers agree that crows are not easily scared. While this "make-believe man" will keep birds away for a time they'll soon be perching on its arms and shoulders.

In the early days the idea was not to scare away crows with this figure of a man, but rather to use it as a cross-symbol that would protect the cornfield. As today, scarecrows were made of two poles fastened together in the form of a cross, considered one of the most powerful charms against evil spirits. Clothes were simply hung on this cross in order to disguise it.

Today we know there's nothing supernatural about a scarecrow. Dr. Ralph Bienfang, an authority on odors, says it's the scent of people on the clothing that keeps these sensitive wild birds away at first. But as rain and wind take away these odors they also take the "scare" out of the scarecrow.

There have been endless superstitions about crows through the ages. You may know this one:

> Crow on the fence,
> Rain will go hence.
> Crow on the ground,
> Rain will come down.

A single crow has always been regarded an evil sign. As a counter-charm some country folks take off their hats when they see one, or bow if they are bareheaded.

The familiar phrase "as a crow flies" means the shortest route from one place to another. Yet studies of migrating crows show they never take the shortest way between two points.

Being one of the more intelligent birds, crows make interesting pets. It's still believed that the bird's tongue must be split in order for it to talk. That's a superstition and a very cruel practice. With a lot of patience on the part of the trainer, most tame crows can be taught to say certain words and to count to three or four.

Swans

"Swans a little before their death sing sweetly," wrote Pliny the Elder about 77 A.D. in his famous works on natural history. But this belief goes back to at least 400 years B.C., when a popular Greek legend told of the soul of the god of music, Apollo, passing into a swan. So swans, it was thought, sang at their death knowing the good things Apollo had in store for them. Today we often refer to the last work of a poet or musician as "his swan song."

Most swans have anything but melodious voices. The whooping and whistling swans are very noisy, while the trumpeter swan of North America is said to be heard two miles away. But some years ago a survey in this country reported, "on rare occasions wounded or dying swans do produce notes which are very different from the ordinary notes of the species and which give rise to the theory that the bird sings before dying." Whether the wounded bird is moaning or singing has yet to be proved. So for the present time this must remain a superstition.

Other beliefs grew up about the swan because of its long life and its faithfulness to its mate. One was that a single swan foretold death.

This graceful bird was no doubt the inspiration for the designs of Viking ships, as well as for the Italian gondola.

Animals

Black Cats

Do you shiver when a black cat crosses your path? Plenty of people do, sure that such an occurrence means very bad luck.

This belief goes back to the Middle Ages when it was thought that a black cat was the companion or mascot of a group of witches, and that it changed into a witch or Satan after seven years of service. Therefore, people reasoned, a cat crossing one's path might be a witch or the Devil in disguise, up to no good.

Those ancestors of ours were amazed at many things about these animals. The gleam of their eyes at night suggested a magic light within. People didn't know, of course, that cats' eyes can't give off light by themselves, but can only pick up light rays and reflect them. This is true of all cats including lions, tigers, leopards, pumas, jaguars and cheetahs.

Another thing that startled these early people was the sparks that sometimes came from a cat's back when stroked. They were sure this was fire.

The cat's ability to land on its feet—though not always—astonished the ancients. This is easily explained now, of course, for slow motion pictures show how this animal rights itself when jumping or falling. The cat has a very flexible spine and every part of its supple body works perfectly together to help it land on its shock-absorbing feet.

The Egyptians who worshiped the cat decided it lived more than once, probably since it was able to survive many dangerous falls. They associated this animal with the Trinity, their sacred symbol of Mother, Father and Son. Three times three, or nine, was the highest expression of honor which could be granted. So today we have the popular saying, "A cat has nine lives."

One superstition with no truth in it is that cats perch on the chests of sleeping babies and elderly

people and suffocate them by sucking their breath.
This may have come from the fact that cats like to
snuggle up to the warmth of human beings. Perhaps
in doing this a cat may have accidentally suffocated a
baby. The idea of sucking the breath probably came
from witchcraft days when the cat was thought to be
an evil spirit.

Sailors like a cat aboard ship, black or otherwise, for
they believe it brings good luck. Also, they consider
this animal a weather prophet. If a cat tears at cushions
and carpets, or moves about uneasily, it is said to be
"raising a wind." This is a half-truth most likely,
since with its alert and sensitive nervous system a cat
probably does feel a wind coming before man does.

It's the black cat's link with witches and the Devil
that makes it a popular symbol of Hallowe'en, "the
night when witches and evil spirits ride."

Do Warts Come from Toads?

There's still a strong superstition that warts are caused
by handling toads and frogs. This is in spite of the
fact that many people have warts who have never
been near these harmless creatures. But perhaps this
fear has kept children from playing in dangerous
swamps and ponds.

The idea, no doubt, began because of the wartlike skin of a toad. For there was a primitive theory that "like produces like." The toad when handled or in pain does emit saliva that irritates a dog's mouth, for instance, causing the toad to be dropped. But this secretion does not produce warts.

One of the many charms supposed to remove a wart is to rub it with a bean or piece of stolen meat. That is then buried in the earth and as it decays the wart is supposed to dry up. Another is to rub a grain of barley on the wart, then feed it to a chicken. The barley's disappearance down the fowl's gullet is a sign the wart will disappear also.

An easy, modern way of curing a wart is by electric needle or X-ray. But since warts may dry up and fall off as mysteriously as they appear, people still like to try their luck at "charming" them.

Toads and frogs are descendants of prehistoric animals. The same superstitions apply to both in spite of their physical differences: the frog has teeth, the toad none; frogs breathe through their skins, toads through their mouths; frogs' legs are longer, and they lay their eggs in clumps instead of in strings.

The ancient Egyptians, Greeks, Turks and Italians looked on the frog as a symbol of inspiration. It's easy to understand why they were amazed at the life history of this creature. They saw the tiny specks of eggs hatch into tadpoles which seemed fish to them. Then they watched with awe the withering of the gills, the development of lungs, and the growth of legs until the tadpole became a frog and could walk on land. So these peoples wore good-luck amulets in the form of frogs.

This charm is still popular today. Also, we use buttonholes called "frogs" on dresses and jackets, a carry-over from the times when frogs were embroidered on clothes to bring luck.

In France three toads or frogs formed the coat of arms of their kings, beginning with Clovis.

Since the French were fond of eating frogs' legs it was a simple step to try frog-medicine. This was usually made from the glands of a frog and was used as a "possible cure" for many illnesses.

The croaking of frogs means rain, say some folks. There may be some truth in this belief for these creatures are sensitive to changes in humidity.

Rabbit's Foot

Do you carry a rabbit's foot for luck? If so, is it always in a left pocket? Are you sure it was the rabbit's left hind foot? And, most important of all, was the animal killed at the full of the moon by a cross-eyed person?

In spite of all these requirements for luck most rabbit-foot charms today are only small front paws. But thousands of people never go out without them. Actors use them for putting on make-up, and kiss them for luck or rub them on their face and hands the night a play opens. Others carry this talisman, believing it can cure certain diseases.

The first fears and superstitions developed about the European hare, a perfectly harmless animal. He's larger than his cousin the rabbit, having powerful hind legs and tips of black on his long ears. Unlike the rabbit who lives in burrows in the ground, most hares live in the open with no home. Also, the young are born with hair and with wide open eyes, while a rabbit's offspring are hairless and blind. However, since most of the habits of these two are alike, superstitions about the hare apply also to the bunny. Both animals are usually called rabbits in this country.

The ancients noticed many things about these timid creatures that they couldn't explain, so thought them both good and evil. They saw how rabbits came out at night to feed, and how they gathered in bands on clear moonlit nights to play as if influenced by the moon. Another astonishing fact was that northern hares were brown in summer and white in winter.

But one thing especially impressed primitive man and that was how the rabbit used his hind legs. There are only two other animals, the greyhound and cheetah, whose rear feet hit the ground in front of the forefeet when running swiftly. Also, rabbits thump the ground with their hind legs as if "speaking" with them. So their hind feet came to be looked upon as a powerful charm against evil forces.

In the early days of witchcraft it was thought a witch could hide in hares and rabbits, and in this disguise harm humans. So, like the folklore about black cats, you never knew when you saw a rabbit whether or not it was really a witch. Even today, some country people say a few kind words of greeting to every bunny who runs across their path, lest harm come to them.

An old tale of a white rabbit playing about under the Easter moon started the custom of giving children a white rabbit at Eastertime. As you know, this is still popular.

Woodsmen look on the rabbit as a weather prophet. They say that if the animal's fur is thick there'll be a hard winter; if thin, a mild one. However, this is not as accurate as some would like to believe, for fur is usually better when an animal has plenty of good food, and not because of any instinct to foretell winter temperature.

Is a White Horse Lucky?

Many believe it's good luck to see a white or gray horse. But in order to make sure that they'll receive a gift they spit over the little finger. However, New Englanders shudder at the sight of a white horse after dark. They quickly lick one thumb and stamp out the impending evil on the palm of the other hand.

The horse has had a leading role in the destinies of mankind, even though domesticated at a fairly recent date. No other animal has so fired the imagination; there have been angel-horses, demon-horses, sun-horses, moon-horses, wind-horses and headless-horses among others. The centaur of the early Greeks, that weird combination of a horse with a man's body at its head, came from impressions formed when Greek warriors first met enemies mounted on horses.

Because the horse finds its way easily in the dark, it was imagined to have the ability to foresee danger. A horse that was white stood for purity. Also people were impressed by the fact that a white horse often lives longer than a black horse. They had no way of knowing then that dark horses absorb the sun's rays and get overheated more quickly than those of lighter colors and so as a rule don't survive as long.

In England, among the country people, there are still two very different beliefs about the white horse. In the northern part, wherever the influence of the Danes lingers, a white horse is looked upon as a bringer of good fortune. This is due to its association with the god Odin's horse, Sleipnir, who was supposed to have had eight legs and to be able to outrun the wind.

But in the Midlands and southern counties, you'll be told to spit over your left shoulder when you see a white horse, since saliva is believed to transform evil into good. This is explained by the fact that those sections of England were laid waste by the Saxons who poured into the country carrying a banner with the sign of the White Horse. So down through the years white horses have been associated in this region with murder.

It is interesting to note that except in the case of albino horses and their offspring a horse is seldom born white. Horses of certain light colors, particularly dappled grays, become lighter and lighter as they grow older until they are pure white.

Bulls and the Color Red

Bullfighting is an ancient sport, a type of it having been carried on by the early Greeks and Romans. Today it is very popular in Spain, as well as in Mexico and other Latin American countries.

Through the years it was believed that a bull becomes enraged whenever it sees red. But many tests made on bulls show that these animals seem to be color-blind. In fact, all animals except man and the monkey are believed to see only some shades of gray. However, tests did prove that a moving object arouses bulls, regardless of its color.

A red cloth or cape was chosen years ago perhaps because it was a favorite color, or because of its brilliance, or because it is the color of blood. But even though the matador wears a bright red costume, it is the waving of his cape that angers the bull.

Man's nervous system is quite different and colors do affect him. The optic nerve reacts most quickly to red and it is by far the most exciting color. The expression, "He sees red!" depends upon this fact rather than on the superstition regarding bulls.

Numbers

"Three" Superstitions

Three has been a mystic number since the world was young. An important reason for this was that primitive man was fascinated by the miracle of birth. Since birth needed three people—father, mother and child—three came to mean life itself. This Trinity was very necessary, the ancients argued, for if life's cycle or civilization was to continue two should always lead to three.

Today we say, "Never two without three," and

"Good or bad things come in threes," meaning that after two happy or unhappy events there's sure to be a third. Both these expressions and another early one, "It never rains but it pours," imply an unconscious fear of the unknown. It's true that certain events do seem to occur in series, but they happen just as often in fours, fives and sixes!

However, because of the importance of the number three since the beginning of time, people even today are relieved when three happenings, such as death, have occurred. For they believe that means the end of a "bad" cycle.

Early man also noted the hundreds of natural groups of three: man as body, mind and spirit; the world as earth, sea and sky; the kingdom of nature as mineral, vegetable and animal. All this strengthened his faith in three as a magic number.

Some of the "three" superstitions and symbols in the Bible and in literature are: Jonah's three days in the whale; Daniel's meeting with three lions; Peter's three denials; Macbeth's three witches.

The phrase, "Three on a match," had an interesting beginning. When a chieftain died in those early days, all the tribe's fires except his were put out. Then the medicine man or witch doctor relit the tribal fires, three at a time, with a firebrand from the chieftain's fire which was believed to contain his spirit.

Centuries later this pagan custom was adopted by the Christian church. In Russia, during the early part of the 10th century, funeral rites included lighting three candles from one taper. This was to help the departed spirit into eternity. Since that ceremony was performed only by priests it became taboo for others to light three candles from one taper or match. This spread to three lamps, three pipes and finally today to three cigarettes. Soldiers are especially superstitious about this last one and for a sensible reason. On a battlefield, three on a match or cigarette lighter may provide light just long enough for an enemy to take advantage.

"Thirteen" Superstitions

If thirteen guests are seated at a table there's only one thing to do to prevent someone dying before the year's up, many people believe. All must join hands and arise as one person. According to superstitious people, this is the counter-charm that undoes the bad luck of thirteen eating together.

This number's taboo can be traced back to the days when man first learned to count. By using his ten fingers and counting his feet as two units he came up

with the number twelve. Beyond that lay the unknown—thirteen!

Before numbers were used, man counted his posses-
sions by using tallies. When he got to twelve he found
he could divide it in half, quarters and thirds. But not
so thirteen. So in due time twelve became a noble symbol to him which accounts for the important use of
"one dozen" throughout the world today.

In spite of this very early opinion, thirteen was regarded as lucky by the ancient Chinese and Egyptians
and still is by people in certain sections of France.
The early Orientals were impressed by the fact that
there are thirteen moons a year. When a "blue moon"
(unusual conditions in the upper atmosphere can cause
a moon to look blue or green) showed up as the last
or thirteenth moon there was great rejoicing, for it
was considered a wonderful sign for the country.
This was a rare happening, of course, and probably
accounts for our saying, "Once in a blue moon."

If you are superstitious about the number thirteen
look at the back of a dollar bill which has been minted
since 1935. The incomplete pyramid has thirteen
steps. The American bald eagle holds an olive branch
with thirteen leaves and thirteen berries in one claw
while in the other he has thirteen arrows. But before
you toss this bill away, remember that these "thir-

teens" commemorate our thirteen original colonies. And that's a very lucky number for millions of Americans today!

Friday the Thirteenth

This is considered the unluckiest of days, unless you were a "thirteenth-of-the-month baby." Then this should be your best day.

The origins of Friday superstitions are many. One of the best known is that Eve tempted Adam with the fatal apple on Friday. Tradition also has it that the Flood in the Bible, the confusion in the Tower of Babel, and the death of Jesus Christ all took place on Friday.

But long before the Bible was written, Friday was considered an important day. Primitive peoples set it aside as a special time to worship their deities and ask them for good crops, health and happiness. Those who worked on this day were told not to expect "good luck" from the gods. Even today many people will not start a trip, move to another house, or begin anything important on Friday because of this antiquated fear.

Later, Friday became the Sabbath of many peoples. The old Jewish lunar calendar gave Friday as the sev-

enth day of the week, and it was many years before
Saturday was made their Sabbath. Friday is still the
Sabbath of the Mohammedans.

In pagan religions Friday was set aside for the cele-
bration of marriage and it was customary to eat fish
on that day. Later, this became a custom of the Jews
and early Christians, except that the day became one
of fasting and humility instead.

The day Friday was named after Frigg (or Frigga),
the Norse goddess of marriage. Later she was confused
with the goddess of love, Freya, who in turn became
identified with Friday. When the Norsemen and Germanic tribes became Christians Freya was supposed to
have been banished to the mountains as a witch. Friday
came to be called "witches' Sabbath." For it was believed that on this day each week twelve witches and
the Devil met—thirteen evil spirits up to no good!
This is one of the reasons for today's superstition
about Friday the 13th.

Sudden Silence

If there's a sudden silence in a group talking together
someone is sure to say, "It must be twenty minutes
after . . ."

This superstition is purely American in origin for

it refers to the death of Abraham Lincoln. It was believed that he died at 8:20 o'clock, and that afterwards, through some supernatural power, a sudden silence would occur at twenty minutes past any hour. The truth of the matter is that President Lincoln was shot about 10:10 in the evening and died the next morning at 7:22.

Another explanation of this belief is that the man who painted the first wooden clocks to hang in front of jewelry stores commemorated the fatal hour of Lincoln's death. But here again the truth is that such wooden clocks were over shop doors long before the President died. Actually, hands of advertising clocks were, and are still today, often placed at about 8:20. This arrangement is pleasing to the eye and leaves space for advertising.

Religious people, long before the above myths came into being, were awed by a sudden silence. Some believed it meant an angel was passing by. Others thought it meant someone was dying, for since the beginning of time silence has been associated with death. So today we have the custom of observing a few minutes of silence in reverence for those who have died.

There is an odd fact that strengthens the superstition about "sudden silence." For when it occurs in a group of people, it actually often is twenty minutes to or twenty minutes after the hour—in spite of the law of averages. Or perhaps we remember the occasion when this happens and forget those when the time is otherwise!

Money

Money Superstitions

"Carry a coin for luck," is often heard. Some people prefer a large, old-fashioned penny. Others depend for luck upon a silver dollar, since silver is a symbol of the moon which controls tides and therefore is supposed to invite growth and prosperity. Women often wear one or more coins on a bracelet.

There are many money superstitions most of which you may know. When giving a purse or billfold be sure to tuck a penny inside so the new owner "may never be without money." Finding a penny means more will follow. Keep a jar of pennies in your kitchen for luck. If the bridegroom gives the bride a coin and she wears it in her shoe at the wedding, the marriage will be happy. Turn a piece of silver in your pocket on seeing a new or full moon if you want your wish to come true.

A coin with a hole in it is considered an especially lucky charm. This superstition began long before money was made, when people believed that a shell or stone with a hole in it had been worn by the god of the sea. So wearing one around the neck kept away evil spirits, and was also a charm against drowning. When coins came into use these beliefs were transferred to them. You'll see Oriental coins today which are round with a square cut out in the center. These are symbols of the round sky and square earth.

Perhaps you've been told never to refuse to give money to a beggar. This fear goes back to the days when a beggar's curse was thought important. It was the custom during the Middle Ages to give coins to the first person seen on coming out of a temple, especially on the eve of a journey or wedding. Poor people stood near the doors to receive these coins. In time this led to the professional beggar who cursed any person who did not give him something. So superstitious people today give money to every "panhandler" lest he curse them under his breath and this curse bring them bad luck.

Flip a Coin

Tossing a coin to decide who owns an object or who is right in an argument is a very old custom. In the beginning people believed it was the gods who made the decision. Today, superstitious people call it Fate, or Lady Luck.

This method of settlement suggests that both people are "good sports." Through the years it has proved to be one of the easiest ways to decide a dispute.

Coin-flipping was especially popular at the time of Julius Caesar. His head was on every Roman coin. In an argument, someone flipped a coin and if the head turned up the person who'd chosen it was right. And so powerful was Caesar that the decision was final. Today you often hear the old saying, "Heads you win, tails you lose."

The custom of tossing a coin into the air with a flip of the thumb is popular with all who believe in "luck." Gamblers and others usually carry their own special coin, believing that it has a better chance of flipping right for them.

Two-Dollar Curse

Here is one of the few native American superstitions—the notion that a two-dollar bill brings bad luck. This idea, it's believed, was started years ago by gamblers. Since a two-spot was the lowest value in cards it was called a deuce, which became a slang word for Devil and thus meant bad luck. So a two-dollar bill came to be scorned likewise.

To take away the "curse," gamblers tore off a small corner of the bill. But why a corner? Because that forms a triangle and thus is a symbol of the number three. This "magical" number has always been considered excellent counter-magic. You'll often see a two-dollar bill with all four corners torn off. The fifth person getting it is supposed to tear it up.

Some people, especially cashiers in restaurants, either pretend to or actually kiss each of these bills they receive. Most aren't aware that this old custom is from the days when saliva was looked upon as the most powerful of counter-charms.

Nowadays, when giving a two-dollar bill in change a cashier often asks, "Do you mind?" In spite of this popular superstition the United States Treasury goes right on printing these bills, for they cost half as much to make as two one-dollar bills. Besides, the Treasury doesn't recognize the "curse"!

Work

Luck in Business

If the first customer who comes into a shop in the morning doesn't buy something, no matter how small, business will be poor the rest of the day, say superstitious shopkeepers. Charms of all kinds have been used through the years to help business prosper, among them a four-leaf clover, rabbit's foot, lucky coin, and a luck-stone with a hole in it. On the stock exchange, a necktie worn by someone during a successful sale may be put on every day thereafter until it is in shreds. Other businessmen have lucky hats, shoes or rings. All these charm-objects help the wearer to have confidence—an important item in business.

The ancients used such mascots as a bee, deer's tooth, or cricket which they believed brought luck if they traded honestly. Otherwise, the gods and goddesses who protected animals would punish them by causing their business to fail.

Many people will only begin a venture at the time of the new moon, a symbol of growth, unless it falls on Friday or the thirteenth of any month.

Long-time leases came about because of the superstition that it's unlucky to move a business from year to year. These leases are usually for an odd number of years, because in material things "even" numbers were once considered to be under evil influence. So we have a ninety-nine-year lease instead of one for a hundred years.

The shaking of hands to bind a business deal was an early custom. The two hands formed a cross, the powerful sun symbol of life and good fortune.

Men of the Sea

Probably there are no more superstitious people than sailors and fishermen. Their fears in the early days are understandable, for they were sure there were sea monsters and other terrible things to meet. Even today, the ocean's unpredictable ways make it seem mysterious.

"Fisherman's luck" still is thought to depend upon many ancient superstitions. When the first fish caught is tossed back into the water it's because of that remote practice of offering the first catch as a gift to Neptune, god of the sea. Inserting a coin in the cork float is another way of giving a present to the sea spirits. Spitting on bait comes from the belief in the "magical" power of saliva. Horseshoes are nailed to the masts of fishing boats for good luck.

Perhaps you've heard this rhyme:

> When the wind is in the East,
> Then the fishes bite the least;
> When the wind is in the West,
> Then the fishes bite the best;
> When the wind is in the North,
> Then the fishes do come forth;
> When the wind is in the South,
> It blows the bait in the fish's mouth.

All sea-going fishermen watch to see how the cod is running in order to foretell weather. One favorite codfish belief is that its ear-stones, called otoliths, will bring good luck. These white irregular, stone-like objects are found in nearly every fish's internal ear, but those of the codfish are considered especially lucky. The ancient belief was that these kept the fish afloat. So, men reasoned, if it worked for the fish it should work for whoever wears or carries them.

Sailors have hundreds of superstitions. You'll see them with a copper wire about their wrist like a bracelet to keep away rheumatism. Or carrying a tiny potato long after it has shriveled to prevent disease. The tail fin of a shark is nailed on the bowsprit of a ship for good luck. Many sailors still like the old superstition of the sea that there's someone who watches over them called "Cherub that sits up aloft."

Ships are never launched on a Friday if it can be helped, for many seamen then won't work on them. For this reason, most vessels carry a metal plate telling when and where the launching took place. At one time a ship was christened with human blood so the sea-gods would have their share and would spare the blood of the men aboard. Animals were sacrificed at a later time, and finally red wine came to be used. Today champagne is popular. But woe to the future of the ship if by any chance the bottle doesn't break over the bow!

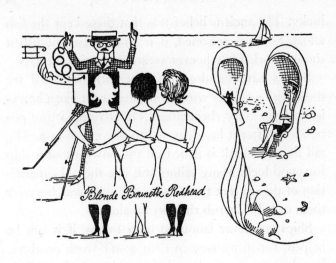

Blonde Brunette Redhead

Character

Blonde, Brunette or Redhead

Light-haired girls are fickle, prove to be false friends,
and "gentlemen prefer blondes." Dark-haired girls are
sincere, have better health, and "men marry brunettes." A redhead is emotionally unstable, has a terrible temper, and "deserves to be burned as a witch."

You've heard these and many like superstitions, for
through the ages people have insisted that character
can be told by the color of the hair. This in spite of
the fact that there are far too many shades between

light blonde and black hair to make any conclusions possible. And who of you doesn't know sincere blondes, fickle brunettes and good-natured redheads? Yet these notions persist.

Many superstitions about hair began because of the belief that "like makes like." Red meant fire to most of our ancestors and so a redhead just had to have a fiery disposition. The ancient Egyptians, Greeks and Romans regarded everyone with red hair as very unlucky. It was during the Middle Ages that redheads were called witches and sometimes burned at the stake. But unpopular as red has been in the past, at the moment it is the favorite hair dye.

There are other hair superstitions besides those dealing with color. A great deal of hair or a hairy body was supposed to be a sign of great strength, which we know to be false. That a girl's long hair saps her strength when she is ill has turned out to be just an old wives' tale. Women with hair on their faces are still thought to have masculine traits. But science says this is caused by upset glands and hormones.

There's an old adage, "Pull out one gray hair and ten will grow in its place." This is impossible, for only one strand of hair can grow from each hair bulb. Also, the case of shock or grief turning hair white in a single night has never been proved.

In sun-worship times, offerings were made to the

rays of the sun, believed to be its hair. Since it was supposed that the sun, like other fire, could do harm as well as good, men offered their hair to be burned hoping to please the sun-god. In certain sections today hair combings are burned because of the old notion that a bird may weave them into a nest and so make the owner insane.

Have you heard the superstition that a woman with a V-shaped hairline, called a widow's peak, will lose her first husband and marry again soon after? This notion came about through a change in the color of mourning clothes. Black had been used for centuries, but during the early Middle Ages white became popular and still is with the Chinese. Then in 1498, young Anne of Brittany decided to wear black at the death of her husband Charles VIII. The next king, Louis XII, married her soon afterward, making her queen of France for the second time.

Hat designers of the time took advantage of the new mourning color to create an attractive V-shaped, or peaked, bonnet of black and white for semi-mourning. This suggested the V-shaped hairline some women have, so that came to be known as a widow's peak. Its association with Queen Anne led to the belief in two marriages. But today, instead of it being thought a warning most women consider a widow's peak a sign of beauty.

Your Name

Names have always been important to people. When first given to individuals, animals and places they were chosen carefully with a hope of endowing whatever was named with some sort of magic. It meant a great deal in those days to have the "right" name. It still does, but mainly now because of each person's mental attitude toward his own name. If you like what you are called and it gives you confidence it's the "right" name for you.

Because of the ease in changing one's name, thousands of foreign-born and native Americans have taken other names for both personal and business reasons. All changes are made with the hope of finding a substitute that will bring happiness and good fortune. The French and Chinese often give children a "milk name" which is temporary so that youngsters may choose their own later.

Name superstitions run into the hundreds. It's lucky to have only seven letters in either first or last name. Men with thirteen letters should add one for good luck. No girl should marry a man whose last name has the same initial as hers, or, as the rhyme goes, "Change the name but not the letter, marry for worse instead of better." A girl whose name is Mary begins with a good start in life.

There's a superstitious fear among some people of mentioning the name of a dead person. The origin of this was that primitives thought a person's name was as much a part of him as his eyes, arms or other parts of the body. To mention his name might disturb his ghost. Even now you'll notice that many people using a dead person's name will say "May he rest in peace," or "Bless his soul," or some other such saying.

Naming a child after a living person was not popular at one time as it was believed this meant death for one or the other. Some religions still forbid this. But as centuries passed the custom reversed itself. Now it's a fairly popular custom to name a baby after a living grandparent, under the superstition that this name will assure the child a long life too.

In introducing two people, modern custom says that the more important person should be named first. This goes back to oldest times when the chief of the tribe or king had to be mentioned by name before others. His name was supposed to have supernatural power.

Dimples

You've probably heard the saying, "Dimple on the chin, the devil within." To some this indicates fun or mischief, while to others it means a bad temper. However, dimples are considered marks of beauty and are very popular with fiction writers when describing both heroines and heroes.

An old rhyme goes like this:

A dimple in your cheek
Many hearts you will seek;
A dimple in your chin
Many hearts you will win.

As you know, a dimple is simply a slight dent in the surface of the body caused by the adherence of the skin to deeper tissues. But early men, knowing none of this and seeing that only certain people had dimples, were sure they meant a magical power of some sort.

In recent years it's been said that a man with a dimple in his cheek or chin will never commit murder. But there's no foolproof evidence to show that a dimple makes any difference in the way people act.

Are Fat People Happy?

The old expression "Laugh and grow fat" leads many to believe that fat people are always happy. One reason for this saying may be that the extra fatty tissue under their skin makes their frowns and worry lines less noticeable. But psychologists claim that overweight people are usually far from happy.

Sometimes the glands or chemical make-up of the body need medical attention. Or, excess weight may be due to upset emotions caused by a lack of love, a feeling of not being wanted, or some frustration.

Another popular saying is, "Fat people are lazy." But we know now that laziness affects fat and thin alike. A fleshy person appears lazy because his movements are slowed up by the weight he carries. Hundreds of seemingly lazy people, both thin and fat, have been cured when fitted with the proper eyeglasses. Others have gained energy after they have had medical care.

A third fallacy in regard to fat people is that there are more fat boys than girls. But statistics show the number is about equal.

Do Hands Foretell the Future?

Palmistry is an ancient art, the study of hands having been traced back to around 5,000 B.C. It was especially popular during the Middle Ages until the Church frowned on it because of its pagan origin. Then its practice was taken over mainly by gypsies.

The left hand is usually the one read, although both may be consulted. Each line, cross or mount has a meaning, many relating to myths of primitive times. Very few expert palmists (many of whom are sincere) can agree as to their exact meanings.

Modern science does not recognize palmistry. The reading of mystical meaning into a line, curve or mark of the hand is considered a very dangerous superstition. Some of the states have laws prohibiting this, teacup reading and other forms of attempting to foretell the future.

However, people still flock to palmists, who are excellent readers of character and who sometimes by chance hit on events that do take place. Having someone talk to us about the most fascinating of subjects—ourselves—has a great appeal. This is especially so of people who feel insecure, or those who are sad or lonely.

Today's use of fingerprints as a scientific way of identification is well known. No two people have exactly the same markings, and these lines do not change during one's lifetime.

Gems

Is the Opal Unlucky?

Many people today refuse to wear an opal because of the superstition that it's an unlucky stone. The ancient Orientals, awed by the opal's changeable colors, thought it was alive. They believed this gem had a soul much like the person's who wore it. When the owner passed away the opal was supposed to become dull. During the Middle Ages, the brilliant flame inside a true opal was regarded as evidence that the Devil lived there. We know now that the radiance and many colors of this jewel are due to the fact that it is a cracked stone.

The notion that opals dimmed the eyes or made one blind persisted for centuries. One of Sir Walter Scott's novels, *Anne of Geierstein*, featured an opal as an enchanted gem. At first it worked magic for its owner but later she died a tragic death. That strengthened the many opal superstitions.

This stone is said to be lucky if you were born in October. But according to an old wives' tale that's only if you're pure of heart. Actually, the opal's only power is giving delight to its owner, for it is one of the loveliest of precious stones.

Diamonds

A diamond is today's most popular stone for an engagement ring. Its sparkle was supposed to have originated in the "fires of love," so wearing this gem meant love and faithfulness.

Diamonds were first known in the Far East. During the Middle Ages pretty women wore this jewel about their faces, for it was believed this would divert the Evil Eye from their beauty. Sometimes the diamond was imbedded in one nostril or ear lobe. Or a woman might wear this "third eye" dangling over her fore-head from strings attached to her hair.

While diamonds were generally considered good luck a superstition began that very large stones brought bad luck. The world's most famous diamonds have had a long history of theft, intrigue, loss of life and other disasters. These facts strengthened the belief in the minds of the superstitious that large diamonds bring misfortune to their owners.

An interesting notion, popular during the Middle Ages, was that two diamonds can produce a third. It became the custom to set two stones in a ring with the hope that they'd bring forth another.

Today the diamond engagement ring is worn on the fourth finger of the left hand. This custom came from two popular superstitions. The ancients believed the heart to be the center of emotions, especially love, and that it was on the left side of the body. The fourth finger of the left hand was thought by the Egyptians to have a vein running directly to the heart.

Many people today feel that a diamond can never wear out. Yet stones used to make fine glass engravings are worn out in six or eight weeks. It is the truth though, and not a superstition, that "only a diamond can cut a diamond."

Do Pearls Bring Tears?

A strong belief, until the last few years when artificial pearls have flooded the market, has been that these gems bring sadness to the wearer. If a string was broken it was believed that the remaining pearls told the number of tears to be shed. Only people born in June could wear them for luck.

As products of the sea, pearls were associated with the sea-gods in Scandinavian mythology. It was said that the tears shed by their goddess Frigga, which brought back to life the sun-god Baldur, were congealed into pearls. In the Orient these gems were associated with the moon. Pearls too were expected to watch over the "tides in the affairs of man."

In the days before science, pearls were supposed to have magical properties. One reason was because people had no idea why they formed in oysters. Also, it was noted that when worn about the neck, pearls seemed more beautiful. Other proofs of magic seemed to be the fact that these gems lost their luster when exposed to bright sunshine, and that they could be dissolved in certain acids.

Now we know that a pearl begins when a tiny tropical worm, the trematode, or some other foreign particle gets into the body of an oyster. To protect itself from this irritation the oyster secretes nacre, or mother-of-pearl, and coats the intruder, thus making it a pearl. Contrary to belief, all oysters cannot make pearls. Only a certain type of oyster or fresh-water mollusk can produce these gems.

It's true that the warmth of the body causes pearls to appear more radiant. But they are harmed by perspiration. Pearls will disintegrate in acid wine or strong vinegar, as they are the softest of precious gems. So the story about Cleopatra dissolving a valuable pearl and drinking it could have been true!

Romance

Love and Lovers

Young people for centuries have thrilled at the phrase, "Love at first sight." The early Greeks and others had the naive belief that every man and woman belonged to one element and that some great power had divided this into two beings. So forever after they would seek each other in order to be reunited. Legends said that you could be sure it was your "other half" if you felt a distinct shock or love at first meeting.

It's true that some people seem to be attracted to

each other at their first meeting. But "love at first sight" is far rarer than writers and the movies would have you believe. And it has proved no guarantee of a successful marriage.

Another romantic superstition is that a person disappointed in love can die of a "broken heart." Since bygone times the heart has been coupled with all the emotions and especially with love. This belief is still accepted by some in spite of the fact that we now know the chief seat of emotions is in the thalamus, a small area at the base of the brain. The truth is that the heart does nothing except pump blood. It may be affected along with the rest of the body by strain caused by great grief, anger or fear. One's health may be "broken" but not one's heart!

Superstitious lovers never swear by the moon which is considered fickle. This age-old belief is referred to in Shakespeare's *Romeo and Juliet*.

> O swear not by the moon, the inconstant moon,
> That monthly changes in her circled orb
> Lest that thy love prove likewise variable.

The many changes of the moon during the month, and especially the eclipses, terrified the ancients. They were positive the moon could not be depended upon. Fear of an eclipse sometimes drove a person insane. But scientists swear by the moon today. Its phases have been recorded years in advance and the moon never fails to behave as predicted.

The little blue flower known as the bachelor button was very popular with young men in love. For according to the Orientals this flower could foretell a happy marriage. It must be picked early in the morning and not looked at for twenty-four hours. If still fresh and "true blue" it meant that the young man had found the right wife. But if withered, and it often was after all that time in a man's pocket, the wedding plans must be given up. Nowadays, if someone calls another "true blue" he considers him a faithful friend.

In olden times, as today, most young girls hoped to be married. So they began filling "hope chests" at an early age. When the household linens were woven, they were put away until the day of the wedding. They formed part of a dowry, which a bride brought to her new husband. At one time a young man was allowed to inspect the "hope chest" and if not to his liking he could call off the wedding.

An old Greek custom was that the sons of a family had to remain single until all the daughters were married. So when these young men fell in love they helped fill their sisters' hope chests in a hurry!

Hope chests are still popular, especially in Europe. But in this country many girls assemble only a trousseau of pretty clothes.

Brides, Grooms and Weddings

June is the favorite month for weddings. In Roman mythology, Juno who was the goddess of women was supposed to bless weddings that took place in what was considered her month. But May was unpopular since the goddess of that month, Maia or Majesta, was the patroness of old people.

"Happy is the bride the sun shines on," is still a popular saying. This is from the old belief that the sun's light would bring many children and therefore a happy marriage. In England, until about 1550 A.D., the wish for the sun on this important day had a practical angle as well. For all marriages followed the Far East custom of taking place outside, usually at the church door. Since England has more than her share of fog and rain, a bride felt very lucky to have the sun shine on her wedding day.

Most brides prefer white for their wedding gowns, the traditional color for hundreds of years. There's an old verse that goes like this:

> Married in white, you have chosen aright;
> Married in red, you'd better be dead;
> Married in yellow, ashamed of the fellow;
> Married in blue, your lover is true;

> Married in green, ashamed to be seen;
> Married in black, you'll ride in a hack;
> Married in pearl, you'll live in a whirl;
> Married in pink, your spirits will sink;
> Married in brown, you'll live out of town.

In spite of these superstitions many modern brides wear the most becoming color, especially at a private ceremony. But there is a rhyme that most brides follow:

> Something old, something new,
> Something borrowed, something blue.

In England they add a line, "And a sixpence in her shoe."

The something old is usually clothing which belongs to an older woman who is happily married. Thus the bride will transfer that good fortune to herself—more "sympathetic magic." Something borrowed is often some relative's jewelry, for this item should be golden. Gold indicates the sun which was once thought to be the source of life.

Brides have worn orange blossoms from time immemorial, for the orange tree is an evergreen and believed to stand for a couple's everlasting love. Because this tree bears blossoms and fruit at the same time the Orientals have always considered it very lucky. In some European countries, brides who wanted large

families wore wreaths of corn or wheat, both emblems
of fertility.

There are several possible origins for the custom of
wearing wedding veils. It may have come from the
Far East custom of Purdah in which women were covered except for their eyes until their marriage day.
Or, the veil may have been a relic of the bridal canopy
held over the heads of the bride and groom as a protection from the Evil Eye.

The bride's bouquet is usually decorated with ribbons in which knots have been tied. Wishes were
supposed to be held by a knot, so many knots were
needed to hold all the good wishes of the bride's
friends.

The "lover's knot" has been an emblem in marriage from remotest times, for it stood for love and
duty. The actual tying together of two pieces of cord
or ribbon at the marriage ceremony is an old Danish
custom which spread to Holland and England. The
knot was symbolic of oneness or unity. Today's expression "the knot was tied" means a marriage has
taken place.

The girl catching the bride's bouquet will be the
next one married. She must make a wish for the
bride's good fortune which will come true, they say,
as she unties one of the knots. In France, instead of

her bouquet, the bride throws one fancy garter. Whoever catches it will marry within a year.

The custom of having bridesmaids and groomsmen, or ushers, probably evolved from the old Roman law which required ten witnesses at a wedding. They were there for one reason—to outwit any bad or jealous demons! The bridesmaids dressed like the bride and the groomsmen like the groom. In this way evil spirits who were envious of such happiness would be confused and not know which two were being married.

"Thrice a bridesmaid, never a bride" is related to the belief "Never two without three." But it was thought the jinx could be broken by being a bridesmaid seven times. For as the moon changed every seven days, so a seven-times bridesmaid might expect a "change" in her bad luck.

The best man stems from the earliest times when a bridegroom captured his bride by force. It was necessary to have a good friend to fight off relatives while the young couple got away.

Wedding rings probably came from the Egyptians. To them a circle meant eternity, a good symbol for a lasting marriage. They were the first to have the notion that there's a vein called "love's vein" which runs from the heart to the fourth finger on the left hand. Later, a Roman scholar wrote that the wedding ring must always be worn on that finger, to keep love from escaping from the heart. Because of this super-stition some wives today never remove their wedding rings.

In ancient Egypt gold rings were used as money. So when today's groom states, "With all my worldly goods I thee endow" he is merely repeating what Egyptian bridegrooms said very truthfully thousands of years ago.

Kissing the bride after the ceremony is an old cus-tom that's still popular. The groom is first and his kiss is to seal the sacred pledges just made. If the bride is superstitious she'll cry, or at least pretend to, for if she doesn't her married life may be full of tears.

Any girl who sleeps with a piece of wedding cake under her pillow is supposed to dream of her future husband. Where this idea came from no one knows. But there was an old Roman custom of breaking a sort of cake over the head of the bride. This was supposed to bring her happiness and wealth. Each guest picked up a piece of this cake in order to have a little bit of that good luck themselves. Following this custom, today's guests are usually given a piece of the wed-ding cake to take home.

The modern bride cuts the first piece of her cake to insure a happy marriage. The groom places his hand over the bride's as she cuts, a sign that he expects to share her good fortune.

Rice-throwing at weddings is a survival from ancient Hindu and Chinese religious rites. Rice was their chief food and so the symbol of health and prosperity. If showered on newlyweds it was supposed to provide many children, most important in those earlier days. Another reason for throwing rice was to appease any evil spirits that might be around. It was hoped they'd accept the rice as a gift and not bother the bridegroom of whom they were thought to be very jealous.

The custom of a honeymoon—going away from friends and relatives right after the ceremony—stems from those same days when a best man came into being. For after capturing the bride, the husband had to hide her away until her angry family grew tired of looking for her. The actual word *honeymoon* came from the practice of the ancient Teutons. For one month after the marriage, while the moon was going through all its phases, the newlyweds drank mead. This was a kind of wine made with honey.

The act of the bridegroom carrying his wife over the threshold of their new home also comes from the time of primitive man's capture of his bride. But it was the Romans who later gave it a superstitious meaning. A Roman bride was lifted into the house to prevent her from tripping, considered a bad omen if done on one's wedding day. Also, she might forget to enter with her right foot and bring bad luck to both of them.

The shivaree, a rural American custom, is the beating of pans and kettles outside the home of newlyweds. It must go on until the bridegroom tosses out a handful of coins. The original custom was called charivari and was performed by the French from remotest times. While today's noisy act is done mostly to tease the bride and groom, in early France this ceremony was to frighten away demons and evil spirits.

Action

Breaking a Mirror

Break a mirror and you'll have seven years of bad luck is a superstition believed by millions of people. Others are sure it foretells a death in the family within a year.

Centuries before breakable mirrors were invented a shiny surface was considered a tool of the gods. Early man wondered at his reflection in the waters of ponds and lakes. Since he had no scientific knowledge he supposed this to be the soul or "other" self, as he called himself in his dreams. He believed that this "other" self was injured if disturbed in any way.

The first mirrors of the Egyptians, Hebrews and Greeks were of polished metals such as brass, bronze, gold and silver. All were believed to possess magic powers. When glass mirrors were made, the breaking of one meant bad luck to the "other" self. Then, in about the first century A.D., the Romans decided that it meant not only bad luck but seven long years of great misfortune!

Why seven? Well, there were two Roman ideas either of which might have led to choosing that particular number of years. One was that life renewed itself every seven years, a belief not supported by medical authorities. Since a broken mirror meant "broken" health, it was probably thought that one would need seven years in which to recover.

The other belief rested in the phases of the moon which change every seven days. The Romans held the moon responsible not only for the tides of the ocean, but also for the "tides" or ages of man.

There was a practical reason why breaking a mirror aroused fear in the early days. They were very expensive and only the wealthy could afford them. A servant handled them with care because whoever broke a mirror was honor bound to replace it. If a family of moderate means did own one it might easily take seven years of saving to replace it.

Another belief was that when a mirror was broken, it was an effort on the part of the gods to keep the one who broke it from seeing some sad event which would take place in his life. Probably from this came the idea that a death would occur in the family within a year.

There are other mirror beliefs today, all stemming from primitive fears. Some people won't let a baby look into a mirror or it may die before it's a year old. Other families cover all the mirrors in the house after a death in the family. This began with the fear that the soul of a person might enter the mirror and be delayed on its journey to heaven.

Aztec Indians kept devils away from the house by placing a jar of water with a knife in it behind the door. They thought that when an evil spirit entered and saw his reflection in the water with a knife across it, he'd turn and flee. Even today this custom of the pail of water with a knife in it is used in America, especially to protect cattle in barns.

Move Clockwise, and Other Circle Superstitions

Many customs are still with us that stem from those remote days when the sun was worshiped. Among them is doing things clockwise, or from east to west as the sun moves. Housewives beat cream, pancake batter and cake dough "with the sun," or sun-wise.

Card players change their luck by getting up and walking clockwise around their chairs. Maypole dancers skip around the pole in the same direction the sun moves. The ribbons from the pole are supposed to be the rays of the sun, sent forth to honor the return of spring.

In the days before astronomy, the return of the sun at each dawn puzzled and awed men. But even then they understood that there could be no life without the sun. So it was natural that they should worship this "all-seeing eye," and even believe that in circling the earth it created life. Our everyday phrases, "the family circle," and the "family cycle" came from this last idea.

Circles of all kinds became important. A ring about the finger has been a charm for ages. The wedding ring as a sun symbol was supposed to help the marriage last a lifetime.

Egyptian women rouged their lips in the beginning not for beauty but to emphasize the red circle formed by the mouth. Since the mouth was believed the door of the body, this was done to keep the spirit or soul from escaping. Also, it was supposed to keep evil spirits from entering.

When you draw a circle about a date or number you usually do it so you'll remember it. But in early days a number was circled for good luck, and before the days of ink this circle was made with blood. The legal red seal of today comes from this idea, with its star-like points standing for the sun's rays.

Here's an interesting thing about the old expression "Going around in circles," which means that one is confused for the moment. It has turned out to be a half-truth, for experiments show that blind-folded people turn in circles. Small swimming creatures do the same thing. Persons lost in a wood will go around and around, even when they're quite sure they're walking in a straight line. All this seems to indicate that a spiral or circling movement is a universal law of life, a fact that our ancestors must have sensed.

Best Foot Forward

Parents often say to their offspring, "Put your best foot forward," thus advising them to show the best side of their nature or talents. A superstitious bride is careful to land on both feet when jumping out of bed the morning of her wedding. This prevents her from starting married life "on the wrong foot."

But which is the best foot? In primitive times, people had the notion that the right side of the body was the good side and thus free of fears and dangers. The Romans, especially, emphasized the belief that gods lived in the right side of man, evil spirits in the left. Thus the right foot became a symbol of reverence to those gods. Shoes and stockings were always put on the right foot first.

In entering a house the right foot went in first. This was supposed to help the friendly spirit on one's right to enter also. But if the left foot preceded, the evil spirit on the left side hopped in instead. So important was this belief to the Romans that a special guard stood at the entrance of public places to make sure people entered correctly.

The expression, "Let's get off on the right foot," is still used today when discussing how to start a successful venture.

Walking Under Ladders

If you must walk under a ladder there are three things you can do: stop long enough to make a wish, quickly cross your fingers, or, make the "fig" sign. This last is done by closing the fist and thrusting the thumb between the index and middle fingers. Any one of these acts will save you from some terrible disaster, say the superstitious.

Ladders have been a popular symbol in the myths of many countries. They signify both good and evil.

The Egyptians believed them good, for they said it was a ladder that rescued their sun god Osiris when he was imprisoned by the spirit of Darkness. So the ladder became a favorite sign to show the ascent of gods. Small ladders were placed in the tombs of Egypt's kings to help them climb heavenward. Today, miniature ladders are still carried as lucky charms by Egyptians as well as by some Americans.

In other parts of the world, walking under ladders was forbidden for various reasons. One of the most primitive beliefs was that a leaning ladder made a triangle with the wall and floor, a symbol of life. Anyone walking through this Sacred Triangle would be punished by spirits unless counter-charms were used.

Among certain ancient Asiatic countries criminals were hanged from the seventh rung of a ladder which was propped against a tree. Since it was supposed that death was contagious, people were forbidden to walk under that ladder for fear they'd meet the wandering ghost of the one hanged and "catch death" from him.

This superstition of not walking under ladders is really a sensible one, for the ladder may fall over on you or someone up on it may let a tool or other object slip and hit you on the head. In England the popular saying is, "A drop of red paint might fall on you!"

Tripping and Stumbling

Never stumble or trip at the beginning of the day. For this is an evil omen, say superstitious people. Even more important, don't trip over the threshold when entering anyone else's house. For in bygone times that meant you practiced witchcraft and therefore couldn't be trusted.

There are a number of counter-charms for these disastrous happenings. One is to repeat, as you whirl about in three circles, "I turn myself three times about and thus I put bad luck to rout." The turning three times makes a triple magic circle which is supposed to give one the chance to begin anew.

Another way of undoing the evil is to go back and pass the place where you tripped, without stumbling again. Some people snap their fingers to scare away the bad spirits who made them lose their balance.

There's one stumble that our ancestors thought meant good luck. That was tripping into one's own home, unless it happened to be one's wedding day. From this superstition we have a saying today that indicates success, "He fell into it."

Photograph Upside Down

Have you ever turned the picture of someone you were angry at toward the wall or upside down? If so, you were probably hoping that person would be punished so he'd be sorry for what he'd done. You might even mean you never wanted to see him again.

This type of superstition comes from an ancient form of performing so-called evil magic. It was thought that turning a photograph of someone toward the wall or upside down would cause evil spirits to punish that person. That notion explains why primitive peoples still refuse to have their pictures taken. They're afraid that the one who gets their likeness may harm them through magic.

This has led to another fear—fear of letting any belonging fall into the hands of someone who dislikes you. Even some civilized people today are afraid that if another has control of some personal belonging that person can "hex" them.

The common phrase, "She turned him down," began during our Colonial days. A suitor, too bashful to propose, would place a "courting mirror" face upward on a table near his lady love. But first he'd look into it, believing the old mirror superstition that by so doing his likeness would remain on the glass. If the young woman wished to accept him she'd lift up the mirror and smile at his "face." If she placed the mirror upside down on the table "he was turned down." This saying nowadays means any kind of a refusal.

Moving Day

The fear of the "unknown" compels superstitious people to do certain things when moving to a new home so good luck will follow. Many of these beliefs came from remote times when tribes wandered from place to place, and might well be fearful of new enemies.

Among the taboos about moving are: never move downstairs in the same building; a move on Saturday means a short stay; it's bad luck to move on Friday; a rainy day means great unhappiness in the new home. According to moving van companies, every day of the week is unlucky for some reason to someone. This makes it especially difficult around our two great moving days, May first and October first.

It's supposed to be a happy move if one takes along the old salt box and doesn't empty it until the new one has been used. To bring luck to the new home, send a new broom and a loaf of bread there before you arrive.

A pleasant custom is that of having a "housewarming" soon after you're settled. Guests often bring gifts and these are supposed to insure good luck for all the family.

Thumbs Up, Thumbs Down

We think of "Thumbs up" as an expression of recent origin. But the "rule of thumb" was very important during the days of Julius Caesar, and even before that time.

While stories vary as to this rule, this is the accepted version. The Romans were fond of gladiator games. At these, two gladiators met each other in sword-play. When one man fell, the audience could decide whether he should be killed or not. Waving of handkerchiefs meant life, while death was indicated by thumbs being turned down.

The position of thumbs at two important times in a person's life no doubt had impressed the ancients. A baby comes into the world, as a rule, with its thumbs folded down within its hands. Each day, as the child becomes more alert, the fingers of each hand release the thumbs. Hence, "Thumbs up" appeared to these early people as a sign of life.

But when a person dies his thumbs relax and seem to turn into the palms of his hands. So to the Romans, "Thumbs down" meant death.

Several superstitions about thumbs are: an itching thumb means visitors; a thumb that turns back shows you can't save money; pricking the thumb tells you that some evil is coming your way.

Nowadays, the gesture of "Thumbs up" is usually a sign showing success or approval.

Memory

String on Your Finger

When you were a child, did you ever have a string tied about your finger to help you remember? Parents still like that way of helping youngsters to recall something they must do. And very often they use this memory aid themselves!

In the olden days, the string was red and was always tied on a finger of the left hand. This was due to the belief that the heart was on the left side and that it was the seat of all knowledge gained through memory. The phrase "learning by heart" comes from that notion. A red string was believed best because that was the color of magic in folklore.

The habit of string-tying is a hangover from the days when anklets, bracelets, belts, and pieces of cloth were placed about painful parts of the body. For early peoples were sure that if the "spirit of life" was kept in one area, that spot would be cured and the pain kept from spreading. So a string on the finger was supposed to "keep" the thought there, to be remembered later.

Even today some people wear a red string about the neck to ward off rheumatism; keep red yarn in the pocket to prevent nose-bleed; and have a black silk cord to protect against colds. Others wear cloth tied with cords about their shoulders to keep them from illness and also from drowning. But of course all strings and cloths, except tourniquets, are mere superstitions and have no medical value.

One popular belief about memory is that only educated people have good memories. This has been proved false by the feats of primitive people who are illiterate. They've handed down by word of mouth from generation to generation whole sacred books, stories and national codes.

Another belief is that older people can't recall well or remember anything new. But memory experts say that young and old—if they're in good health—can remember if they have a system, plus the desire to work at it. On the whole, you'll remember names, places and things that you have a definite interest in. And without a string tied to your finger!

Forgotten Something?

If you have to go back for something you've forgotten you'll have bad luck all day unless you perform some act of counter-magic. The favorite one is to sit down right after returning. Then count to ten and recite a magic formula, or make a wish. After that you can start out again knowing the so-called jinx is broken.

Sitting down goes back to the idea of the circle, symbol of the sun's course through the heavens. The interrupted journey you were taking—a "broken circle"—is supposed to be rounded out when you sit down. Now you can begin again to make a new circle or journey.

The counting to ten and reciting formulas such as "If I sit, bad luck will flit" are just for good measure. Ten is used because it is twice five, the sacred number for directions.

If you choose to make a wish, this is a favorable time, since by your sitting down evil has been changed into good. But be sure and close your eyes. This last comes from the ancient custom of wishing on the sun. The eyes were closed then, of course, to shut out the glare.

Some people claim that if you haven't time to sit and recite something you can break the jinx by spitting over your left shoulder. Or you can take seven steps backward and whirl around—that "magic" circle again!

The superstition that women forget more often than men seems to be widely accepted. It has so impressed a certain tribe in Madagascar that when a woman's funeral procession is near the grave the attendants return to her home for an hour or so. This gives the woman's ghost a last chance to get anything she might have left behind.

Sleep

How to Sleep Well

"Sleep on your right side" is a saying that can be traced back to when people believed the heart was on the left side of the body. Children and adults were warned that if they slept on their left side the weight of other organs would press on the heart. And a crushed heart meant death!

We know now that although the beat of the heart seems to come from the left side, this organ is just about in the center of the body. It can't be affected by weight from either side. Even when the heart is enlarged on the left side as in certain forms of heart disease, there's still no danger in lying on that side.

Another well-known superstition is that one should sleep with head pointing north and feet pointing south. The feeling was that the magnetic waves flowing from the North Pole to the South Pole helped one sleep well. Even today some people carry a compass when traveling so they'll know where due north is. Modern science laughs at this, saying that there isn't enough iron in the body to be affected in the least by polar magnetism.

Have you heard that a sleepwalker must never be quickly awakened or he may die? This has been proved untrue for years, yet it still remains a popular superstition. Sleepwalking is not due to mental illness, but usually shows that the person has fears, worries or unhappy emotions. Most people outgrow this habit, while others need a doctor's help.

Many people still are of the opinion that a youngster sleeping with an adult loses some of his strength. It's true that two people—of any ages—don't sleep as well together as alone. No one "sleeps like a log," for studies show that you change your position from twenty to twenty-five times each night. Naturally the more room you have to do this in, the more comfortable you'll be. But, except in the case of a baby that might easily be crushed or smothered by an older person, there's no real danger to children who sleep with adults.

In spite of all these notions about sleeping we do know that both mind and body respond to a strong faith in anything. So if you're sure you'll sleep better on your right side or with your body resting north and south, the chances are you will!

Getting Out of Bed Right

You often hear it said about a cross or grouchy person, "He got out on the wrong side of the bed." This is another superstition related to the belief that the right side is the good side; the left side, the evil side.

Therefore climbing out of bed on the left side has meant a bad day ahead since remote times. Hotel bedrooms are often planned with this in mind, beds being placed so that one can't get out on the left side.

A counter-charm for this bad omen is to turn, walk backward into the bed, then start all over again in the correct way.

Does Food Cause Bad Dreams?

Most people place the blame for bad dreams and nightmares on the food they ate the night before. This is a superstition, for food has nothing to do with pleasant or unpleasant dreams. It may be that something you've eaten has given you indigestion. In that case you'll probably sleep lightly and remember your dreams.

Dreaming is perfectly normal for everyone. Most of your dreams will center about you, some being fanciful and others following experiences you've had. Continuous nightmares may show a fear or upset emotion. Sometimes a specialist is needed to help stop them.

Down through the ages, many people have thought there was a supernatural meaning to dreams. But modern psychology has stripped a lot of the mystery from dreaming, although there's still much to learn. Many specialists agree that the true meaning of a dream is disguised in a symbol. This meaning can only be known after a study of the person's past experiences and the associations he has formed in his mind. The same dream, therefore, may have a different meaning for every person. This is in spite of what the "Dream Books" say!

Fear of the Dark

We are born with only two instinctive fears: the fear of falling, and the fear of a loud noise. But many children grow up terrified of the dark, which usually means they have copied parents or friends who have such fears.

Primitive man had every reason to be fearful of the night, living as he did in great forests where there were prowling beasts and other enemies. So it's not to be wondered at that he invented a god of Darkness, as well as many charms to protect himself. From the Chinese the Romans got the idea that there is power in peony seeds. These were worn about the neck to guard against the evils of darkness. Today, we use sensible charms to make youngsters forget their fears, such as night lights or luminous stars and figures on the bedroom ceiling. All are much more effective than peony seeds!

The early fear of darkness made savages believe that the air after sundown was harmful. They claimed that evil air rose from the ground then and floated about everywhere. Today we know this isn't true—

that there's little difference between day and night air. While the sun's rays during daytime are highly healthful, at night there's usually less dust stirring. People who still are superstitious about the night being unhealthy forget that closed windows mean less fresh air, a most necessary item for good health.

Wishes

Make a Wish

Most of us like to wish on the first robin we see in the spring, a load of hay, the new moon, and many other things we've been told make wishes come true. Children everywhere know this saying:

> Star light, star bright,
> Here's the wish I wish tonight.

The first robin and the first star are only two of many "firsts" that are supposed to grant wishes. Other popular ones include the first visit to a new place, and the first ride on a new means of transportation.

Wishing on a load of hay is probably as old as farming itself. For hay was a symbol of a good harvest that would provide for both cattle and farmer.

The new moon has always been thought to be able to grant favors. Many still bow to it three times, or nine times to triple the good luck. Because of the moon's silvery glow people thought it was made of silver. So wishes for good fortune and business were spoken as one shook silver coins in hand or pocket. Today when a man who is trying to reach a decision jingles coins in his pocket he is unconsciously following the age-old superstition of calling upon the moon for help.

You've probably wished at a Wishing Well. One way is to drop a coin in as you make your wish, and wait to see your reflection in the water. Casting money into water comes from the quaint belief that gifts to the sea-gods brought good luck. Honeymooners at Niagara Falls toss coins into the Bridal Veil Falls there and wish for long, happy marriages.

Many believe that a wish made while crossing a short, straight bridge will come true. But they must hold their breath while wishing so as not to swallow an evil spirit. This comes from the time when it was thought that bad spirits could travel only in a straight line over water. Orientals and others built their bridges oval or dome-shaped so the reflection in the water would complete a circle. This circle, symbol of the sun's path through the sky, was the counter-magic to negate any evil. Also it was thought that the good water spirits, who didn't like bridges either, would be pleased since they could travel on an arched bridge. So if you crossed such a bridge your wish would be granted whether you held your breath or not.

In primitive psychology there was much "wishful thinking." Early man expected to get any wish made while looking at or touching something that indicated riches or good fortune. This was based on sympathetic magic, or "like brings like."

Do you know the childish notion about wishing on a dropped eyelash? It was assumed that if an evil doer got hold of another's eyelash he could work magic against him. Therefore, if one fell out accidentally it was always burned. But some say that a dropped eyelash can bring good luck. First you must lay it on the back of your left hand as you make your wish. Then, placing the back of the right hand under the left palm, you must hit the palm with it three hard blows as you close your eyes. If the eyelash is still there the wish won't come true. But if any of the three blows knocks it off, the lash has gone to bring back your wish.

Wishbone

Everyone likes the superstition that if two people make a wish and pull the ends of a dried wishbone, the one breaking off the piece with the head on it will get his wish.

In ancient bird-lore, the hen and rooster were in great favor. Since the hen announced the laying of an egg and the cock crowed at the beginning of day men were sure these fowls must be divine and could answer human questions.

There are records of people consulting "hen oracles" as early as 322 B.C. In one type of oracle a circle was traced on the ground and divided into twenty-four parts for each letter of the alphabet. Grains of corn were placed in the sections. A cock or hen was led to the circle and the first grain picked up indicated the first letter of the name of a future husband. Other questions were answered in the same manner. Then the fowl was sacrificed to a special god. Its collarbone was saved and hung in the sun to dry. The person seeking an answer from this god made a wish on this bone which gave it the name "wishbone." Afterwards two people snapped the dry bone, each making his own wish. It was supposed to be granted to the one holding the longer end, as this was a "lucky break."

The wishbone of any fowl is considered good luck. It's still the custom to wear tiny gold and silver wishbones as pins, charms for bracelets, and on other jewelry.

Luck

Knock on Wood

This is one of the most popular superstitions. You see people knock on wood after boasting, making a prediction, or speaking of good fortune. Some knock three times to make sure Lady Luck hears them!

Since wood comes from trees, this belief goes way back to ancient tree folklore. Down through the ages people believed that trees were the homes of gods. These were kind, obliging gods if approached in the right way. In asking a favor of the tree god one touched the bark. After the favor was granted the tree was again knocked as a sign of thanks.

You probably played "tree-tag" or "wood-tag" as a child. Touching a tree meant you were safe, one of the many beliefs of primitive tree worship.

Another common idea was that spirits who were jealous of human happiness were always nearby. It was supposed that if one knocked on wood these spirits couldn't hear any good news being discussed.

There has always been a strong feeling in all countries that trees and humans are very close. We find the "Tree of Life" mentioned in the Bible and also in ancient Indian legends. Today you trace your family back several generations through what we call the "family tree."

The evergreen was believed to be the favorite of the tree gods. Many people today still follow the custom of planting an evergreen at the birth of a child. This is a nice custom, as long as no one believes this tree has the power to foretell the health of the child or how long he will live.

Cross My Heart

You've probably said many times, "Cross my heart and hope to die," to indicate that you were telling the truth. Usually this is spoken as the index finger makes a large cross over the heart. In long-ago folklore, the heart was believed the seat of wisdom. So it was assumed that the heart knew whether you were lying or not.

Also, the heart has been called the seat of emotions. Today valentines, heart-shaped jewelry and other objects are given to show a feeling of love or friendship. Others considered the heart as the place of memory. We have the popular saying, "Learning things by heart," from this idea.

Still another notion was that the heart meant courage, and young men sometimes ate a lion's heart hoping it would make them fearless. "It gives one heart," meaning courage, is an expression sometimes used.

There are any number of other traditional phrases still popular today. "Have a heart"; "He has no heart"; and, "He's chicken-hearted," all indicate cruelty or cowardice. On the other hand, "He has a heart of gold" is a most flattering compliment.

"Bread and Butter"

Children and many grownups consider it an evil omen if while walking with a friend some object comes between them. It may be a person, tree, or anything large enough to separate them. They believe the friendship will be completely over if something isn't done quickly to break the spell. The most popular way is for both to say, "Bread and butter," as each crosses his fingers.

Another thing that's supposed to wipe out the jinx is to go back to where the separation took place and start walking again together from there. Sweethearts must do this holding hands or they can never be married, according to the superstitious.

You can also counteract bad luck by stopping and making a cross on the sidewalk with your foot. This is thought especially good for three people walking in a row, who wish to change places but not disrupt their friendship. Another charm, less likely to amaze onlookers, is that of simply crossing your fingers.

This power to ward off evil—making a cross either with the foot or hand—was supposed by primitive peoples to form a union and repair the "break through" of the third person or object. The retracing of steps and starting again meant that a "magic circle" had been completed, and that would keep the friendship from being broken. The solemn saying of "Bread and butter" also formed a complete unit since these words belong together. A modern version, "Bread and margarine," is considered effective too.

Cross Your Fingers

Do you cross your fingers when making a wish, believing this will help the wish come true? Or do you tell others, "Keep your fingers crossed for me," when you are planning a new venture?

This gesture came from the idea that the cross was the sign of perfect unity, that when two lines crossed any wish was held at the center of the lines until it was granted.

In the early days two people made this cross by one placing his index finger over the index finger of the other. As the first person wished, the second hoped it would come true. Later, people began forming the cross as we do today by placing the middle finger over the index finger.

Another superstition about crossed fingers is the belief that when two people happen to say the same thing at the same time they have a chance for a wish to come true. They must quickly lock little fingers of the right hand as they are wishing. This forms a hooked cross which will hold the wish. Then each one speaks the other's name. Or if one calls out a word, the other must answer with a word that's closely associated, such as cup, saucer.   From this superstition came the jingle:

> I say chimney, you say smoke,
> Then our wish will not be broke.

There's a belief among children that if they cross their fingers when telling "white lies" these will not count nor harm them. You may have seen a cartoonist use this idea to show that a man's untruthful or deceitful. He'll draw him holding one hand behind his back with the fingers crossed.

Lucky Break

This is an expression often heard today. Where did it come from?

Some think it grew out of circus slang regarding the weather. Since pleasant days are so important to circus business, people said it "broke bad" whenever it rained, snowed or turned cold. Others think this term started in poolrooms, when if a player drove one or more balls into a pocket on his first try it was known as a "lucky break."

But this popular phrase, no matter where it came from, was known as far back as primitive times. When a member of a tribe wished to frighten away an unseen evil spirit he snapped a stick in the middle to make a loud noise. If things went well after that he said it was due to the "lucky break."

Today, snapping a twig or match in two is still used by some people who, like their ancestors, think it will scare away harmful influences. Snapping fingers and knuckles is also a carry-over of this gesture which was once thought so important.

Are Pins Lucky?

You can have your choice of pin superstitions, some bringing good luck and others calamity. Perhaps the best-known belief is:

> See a pin and pick it up,
> All the day you'll have good luck.

This is contradicted by the saying, "Pick up a pin, pick up sorrow." Other expressions are: "Pass up a pin, pass up a friend"; "See a pin, let it lie, all the day you'll have to cry."

Many people believe that to give a pin or any sharp object to a friend will spoil that friendship, unless the other doesn't thank them for it. Other superstitions are: black-headed pins must not be used when having a dress fitted; finding a safety pin means good luck;

a hairpin working loose from the hair shows your sweetheart is thinking of you; pins stuck in a wax image of a person will make him feel pain.

The first pins and needles were thorns, fowl and animal leg bones, and the like. Their use, of course, was in making crude garments and tents. Since most had a shiny surface they fell under the superstition that anything that shone was a means by which magic was worked.

Pins were also connected with the ancient fear of spilled blood. Today most of us put our finger to our mouths when we've pricked it, just as those early savages did. But in their case, it was done so no one could get their blood and use it for evil purposes!

There's a wide-spread notion that a sliver should be removed by a needle, and never by a pin. But science says it makes no difference which you use, as long as it is sterile.

Fashion

Ears and Earrings

"Someone's talking about me," is a common saying when there's a ringing or burning in the ear. If it's in the left ear you're supposed to be well-spoken of; if in the right, someone is speaking evil of you. However, some interpret this superstition the other way around.

There are two quotes for an itching ear: "Left for might, right for spite"; and, "Left or right, good at night."

These superstitions go back to the belief that a sensation in the ears meant a message of some kind. Not knowing that ringing and itching was caused by such things as wax, a foreign body in the ear, or poor circulation, people were sure they foretold something mysterious. One counter-charm was to use the "ear finger," or little finger, to stop the ringing. Another was to make a cross with saliva and then touch the ear, saliva being a guard against evil spirits.

Superstitions for curing earaches were, and still are, numerous. Some are harmless, others quite harmful. For instance, running ears often are not cared for because of the childish notion that it's healthy to let "the mischief run out."

The custom of piercing ear lobes goes back to the days when earrings were worn as amulets to protect one from wicked spirits. A single earring was as popular as two, and at one time these charms were worn by kings, poets and other men. Sailors believed that a pierced ear with a ring through it meant stronger eyesight. Even today some men of the sea wear an earring.

Ears were thought by some of our ancestors to be the seat of intelligence. Children's ears used to be pulled "to make them remember." But we know now that this is harmful.

Clothing Wrong Side Out

If you accidentally put on a garment wrong side out superstitious people say you'll have good luck for the rest of the day if you wear it that way. But few know the weird background of this belief. Clothes were worn wrong side out in remote times as a disguise, so Death wouldn't recognize the owner!

Early man invented all sorts of counter-magic to protect himself against disease and death. He was especially fearful when anyone in his own family died, for he was sure that the spirit of Death might be looking for more victims. So he painted his body with strange designs, and wore his clothes backwards as well as wrong side out. Now no evil spirit would recognize him, he thought. Also, being dressed like this protected other people who would stay away from him and not "catch death."

Mourning veils were worn by women for the same reason, to hide them and protect others. Close relatives of the departed could wear no jewelry or appear in public for weeks afterward in case the Evil Spirit was about. Our mourning customs came from these early fears, but now we observe them out of respect for the dead.

As the centuries rolled on it was decided that when you accidentally put on a garment wrong side out this was a warning from a good spirit or angel. In leaving it on you checked some evil planned against you and brought yourself good luck instead.

Another popular clothing superstition is that of turning one's cap and wearing it backward. This is supposed to ward off bad luck, making it good instead. Women turn their aprons and men pull their pockets inside out for the same reason. But this was not supposed to be a disguise. Rather, it came from that popular early belief that doing something in reverse changes the order of things.

Umbrellas

Umbrellas have been carried in Eastern countries since the eleventh century B.C. But only rulers, chieftains, or members of religious orders were allowed to use them. The umbrella was supposed to protect royal heads not so much from the weather as from evil spirits that might be jealous of great people. In countries where the sun's heat is very intense it's easy to understand why the hot rays were believed to contain hateful spirits. Umbrellas are still used in ceremonies in the East.

When common people were finally allowed umbrellas these were sun shades or parasols. It wasn't until about a hundred and fifty years ago that this device was waterproofed, as a protection against wet weather.

Do you ever carry an umbrella "to ward off the rain"? This belief is from the days when thinking the opposite of what you wanted was supposed to keep a thing from happening. Carrying an umbrella on a threatening day works very well—if the day happens to stay dry!

Early umbrellas always had eight spokes, for thus a double cross was formed—considered a sign of excellent luck. Today, "to doublecross" a person means something quite different.

Fairies

Gremlins, Elves and Leprechauns

The "little people" are some of the most delightful figures of superstitions ever imagined. Every country or section of the world has its favorite tiny folk or fairy. The Germanic peoples gave us elves who are mischievous and often spiteful, and have no souls. From France come the bad-tempered goblins who haunt dark places, and the little bent gnomes who work in mines. Scandinavian folklore offers the troll who can be either dwarf or giant, and who dwells in caves by the sea or up in the mountains. The friendly brownie, according to Scottish belief, lives with families and works for them at night. In Irish folklore it's the leprechaun, a little old man who stands about two feet high. He owns great treasures, but you have to frighten him very much to get anything away from him.

The best part of these small creatures is that they can be blamed for all human ills, bad luck, and accidents. Which is one of the main reasons why they were invented, of course! But none seems to be blamed more than today's gremlin. This little fellow is held responsible for anything bad that happens in an airplane, as well as in a number of other places.

There are many tales about the origin of gremlins. Some say they used to live in hollow banks beside river pools in England. Then they moved to mountain crags. So delighted were they at being up high that they began sneaking rides on airplanes as soon as those were invented.

These little imps clog oil and fuel lines in planes, fog the windows, play merry-go-round on the compass, and drink every drop of gasoline. Pilots aren't very fond of gremlins (except to blame things on), and they don't like their mates, the fifenellas, not to mention their youngsters, the widgets. At high altitudes strato-gremlins, called spandules, take over.

You can blame them for putting ice on the airplane wings.

Fortunately there are all kinds of charms and counter-magic to fight the evil thought up by the small fairies of the world. One ancient counter-charm has actually led to the manufacture of socks with white toes. For the Irish say that such a sock will keep you from being tripped by the "little people."

Witches and Witchcraft

Witches were created by our savage ancestors as part of the pagan religions of mankind. In that early period men sought reasons for illness, death and all the terrible things that happened. Among those held responsible was the Devil. Witches were imagined as women who had a friendly pact with the Devil and did his bidding. Men could be witches, too, but they were often called sorcerers or wizards. All were supposed to have supernatural power in making "black magic."

A witch, the primitives said, was associated with the moon and cast her spells at night. She usually traveled on a broomstick. You could be sure a witch had been around if a baby died (she liked to eat them!), a cow was sick, or the crops were bad. Witches could be blamed for everything.

Twelve of these evil spirits were supposed to meet with the Devil in a meadow or graveyard every Friday which was called "witches' Sabbath." There, these thirteen creatures would plan all sorts of deviltry.

According to pagan faith a witch was able to change her form and she often chose to be a cat, rabbit or pig. Also she could become a person, and this began probably the most tragic of all superstitions. Down through the centuries thousands of innocent people were burned or hanged as witches.

A human witch was supposed to be recognized by many means, such as eyebrows that met over the nose, a birthmark, red hair, or evil-looking eyes. If someone disliked you, or wanted to get hold of your property, it was easy to find a "Devil's mark" somewhere on you!

Some people enjoyed pretending they were witches, as long as they weren't caught by the law. You could consult them secretly for love potions, charms and all kinds of medicines. One "powerful" medicine was made from parts of toads, snakes, insects and black cats.

Probably the witch's most important act was "hexing" or casting a spell on someone. Sometimes she would mix a poison or mumble weird chants. But the favorite way was to make a "witch's doll"—a small wax or clay image of a person—and stick it full of pins.

This, it was claimed, would make the person ill and finally kill him.

Until fairly modern times there were few people who didn't believe in witchcraft. When the churches of the Middle Ages denounced witches as evil spirits there began the terrifying "witch hunts" that lasted until about two hundred years ago. In Scotland alone there are records of 4,000 so-called witches being killed.

The most famous "witch hunt" in this country took place in Salem, Massachusetts, in 1692. It began when a West Indian slave by the name of Tituba scared young girls into fits with her terrifying voodoo tales. The doctor of the town decided that the girls had been bewitched. To protect herself, Tituba accused several women of casting spells. Meanwhile the young girls, delighted by all the attention, screamed and rolled on the floor to make believe they were bewitched. So hysterical did the townspeople become that before it was over twenty-two innocent people had died, nineteen of them hanged.

All primitives in the world still believe in this pagan faith. In parts of Africa today the "witch doctor" and his voodoo practices are common. "Medicine men" claim to heal by magic. Hexing is still done by means of the "witch's doll."

This last has caused illness and even death in some

cases. But we know now that these were due to the power of suggestion. If people keep saying that something's going to happen to you, and through fear you believe them, it sometimes does happen. Not because of what they say or the pins stuck into a clay figure, but because *you believe it*. For psychiatrists tell us that anything we have strong faith in, whether it be good or evil, can affect us physically.

There are many people in this country who believe in witchcraft today, either through ignorance or fear. Every few years a murder is committed by someone who thinks he's been "hexed" by another. In parts of Louisiana they talk about the terrifying werewolf, supposed to be a person in the form of a wolf.

As in olden days, the superstitious use many counter-charms. Salt, bread, and spitting over the left shoulder are popular. For curing a child or adult who is ill, or who is thought to be under someone's spell, there are certain chants or mumbo-jumbo to be muttered. In the Dutch section of Pennsylvania most barns are painted the "magical" color of red, each building bearing a "hex sign" to frighten away evil spirits.

If you happen to be afraid of witches try the counter-magic of placing a broom across your doorway. No witch, it is said, can ever resist a broomstick. So she'll hop right on yours and fly away!